The End of the American Gospel Enterprise

Other Books by Michael L. Brown

It's Time to Rock the Boat:
A Call to God's People to Rise Up
and Preach a Confrontational Gospel

Our Hands Are Stained With Blood:
The Tragic Story of the "Church" and the Jewish People

Whatever Happened to the Power of God?
Is the Charismatic Church Slain in the Spirit
or Down for the Count?

How Saved Are We?

Compassionate Father or Consuming Fire?
Who Is the God of the Old Testament?

Yeshua: Who Is He? (mini-book)

Available from:
Messiah Biblical Institute Bookstore
P.O. Box 7163
Gaithersburg, MD 20898-7163

For information on Messiah Biblical Institute and Graduate School of Theology, or for a listing of other books and tabes by Michael L. Brown, write to:

Messiah Biblical Institute
P.O. Box 7163
Gaithersburg, MD 20898-7163
(301) 330-6006

The End of the American Gospel Enterprise

By Michael L. Brown

Destiny Image Publishers
P.O. Box 310
Shippensburg, PA 17257

"Speaking to the Purposes
of God for this Generation
and for the Generations to Come"

ISBN 1-56043-002-8

For Worldwide Distribution
Printed in the U.S.A.

Destiny Image books are available through these fine distributors outside the United States:

Christian Growth, Inc. Jalan Kilang-Timor, Singapore 0315	Successful Christian Living Capetown, Rep. of South Africa
Lifestream Nottingham, England	Vision Resources Ponsonby, Auckland, New Zealand
Rhema Ministries Trading Randburg, South Africa	WA Buchanan Company Geebung, Queensland, Australia
Salvation Book Centre Petaling, Jaya, Malaysia	Word Alive Niverville, Manitoba, Canada

Contents

Foreword

There is not much that has been written in recent years that has stirred me. This book stirred me. I read it with great profit. It is vibrant and has an anointing.

Mike's writing is bold but not brash, incisive but not insulting, alert but not acrimonious, daring but not damning. I believe Mike heard a word from the Lord, an echo of mercy from the voice of God.

I recommend that this book be read publicly, two chapters at a time without comment, in the mid-week service of every evangelical church in the nation. If they will do that in each church, it could shake the whole country.

Jesus came to send fire on the earth (Lk. 12:49-50). We need a baptism of fire today to consume our carelessness and erase our effete efforts; to send us with burdened hearts, burning lips, and brimming eyes to a dying generation.

Read this book and be ignited. Then go and be an igniter of others.

Leonard Ravenhill

Preface

This book represents the culmination of seven years of consuming hunger for the glory of God. It articulates the cry of my heart and the longing of my soul. It shares the burden of my life. *It is high time for us to awake from our slumber!*

For seven years now the word of repentance and the promise of revival has been my meat and drink. Too many times God's holiness has been violated. Too often His Spirit has been quenched. Time and again His people have fallen short. Now He is saying, "Enough! You must get right with Me while there is still light. I am ready to send the flood."

In July of this year, while on a personal prayer retreat, God moved on me to begin to write. Within a month's time, the book was finished. I now deliver it to you.

My heartfelt thanks go to some dear friends who have played an important role in helping see this book through: to Michael Murray and to Ari and Shira Sorko-Ram, for carefully reading the manuscript and making many valuable suggestions; to Dr. Joe Femino in New York and to Pastor Walter Healey (Church of Grace and Peace, Toms River, New Jersey) for helping to underwrite the initial cost of publication; to my fellow-soldiers here at Beth Messiah Congregation, for praying and standing with me; and to Leonard Ravenhill, a senior statesman in the Body, for graciously offering to write the Foreword. In the past his writings deeply impacted my life. And now, over the last few weeks, his friendship has given me a revelation of eternity.

This book could not have been written without my wife Nancy. She refuses to let me be satisfied with anything less than the true glory of God and will never let me compromise. Some years ago she challenged me with an exhortation from John Lake. Let me leave you with his words: "Beloved, for the sake of a dying, suffering world, pay the price, get God's power, and set the prisoners free."

May God be glorified through this work!

Michael L. Brown
October 1989

Note to 1993 edition: Although the entire book has been re-typeset, this is an exact reprint of the original 1989 edition, with the exception of a few typos which have been corrected and a few sentences which have been changed.

Introduction

America needs to repent!

Few believers would disagree with these words. Our country has fallen headlong into sin. Drug abuse and pornography are everywhere, murder and rape abound, and the family has been all but destroyed. Millions of unborn babies have been butchered for money, and little children tortured and killed. Perversion has become an alternative life-style, and almost all fear of God is gone.

But where is the Church of America? With all of our conferences on spiritual warfare and intercession how are we changing our nation?

Every two seconds a violent crime or theft is committed. Three babies are aborted every minute. Ten women are raped every hour (this does not include the thousands of other rapes that are never reported). Fifty-six people are murdered every day. Our gospel has not affected the streets!

A nine year old boy eating breakfast saw a girl riding a snowmobile outside his window. He got his father's rifle, fatally shot her as she rode by, and returned to eat his cereal. What has happened to conviction? *We have become a people without a conscience.*

Four hundred teenagers commit suicide every month; ten thousand more try each week. Our church youth programs have hardly touched them or given them a reason to live.

The porno industry makes nine billion dollars a year. How much of that money comes from believers?

Over twenty-five million Americans admit to illicit drug use; more than ten million are acknowledged alcoholics. The devil is taking men and women captive faster than we are setting them free. Recently a father was arrested for allowing another man to rape his daughter in exchange for crack.

More than four million couples now live together out of wedlock, and courts have recognized homosexual "marriages." But the Church has little to boast about. The divorce rate among believers is as high as the divorce rate in the world, and pastors in every denomination have been caught in adulterous affairs and homosexual activities.

Four million of our countrymen are child molesters. One of them sexually abused three hundred eighty children before he was caught. Ministers and Sunday School teachers have been arrested on similar charges.

Yes, America needs to repent. *But the state of the nation is the fault of the Church, and as God's judgments fall, they will first be falling on us.*

America needs to repent.
The judgments of God are here.
His people are being shaken.
Can your house stand?

Chapter 1

The Backslidden Church of America

At this very moment, there are more believers living here in the United States than at any time in history. Hundreds of churches boast memberships in the thousands, and dozens of ministries claim to be touching the world. Gospel radio and television shows are aired 24 hours a day and Christian literature pours off the presses at an unprecedented pace. Believers are neck deep in praise tapes and teaching materials.

But something is terribly wrong. Our society is crumbling all around us. Fear of God has all but disappeared. The world sins with apparent impunity. And the people of God say, "We're blessed!"

Something horrible has taken place. *The Church has backslidden without even knowing it.* Like Sardis, we have become the "perfect model of inoffensive Christianity" (G. B. Caird), "having a reputation of being alive, yet being dead" (Rev. 3:1). Like Sardis, we have so to come to terms with our pagan environment that we provoke almost no opposition and make virtually no impact. And like Sardis, situated high on a mountain rock, we have felt safe and secure in this world.

Why else has persecution ceased? How else do we explain the fact that Americans can sin so much with so little guilt—unless we have ceased to be the "salt of the earth and the light of the world" (Mt. 5:13-16), unless we have ceased to be the standard of righteousness for our society. Paul taught that "where there is no law, there is no transgression" (i.e., law breaking; Rom. 4:15). Do the people of the world know that they are breaking God's law when we have not lived it out and proclaimed it? Can we accuse them of "irreverence" when we have shown them nothing to revere?

The fact is, we have gotten so fat that we can't even get out the church doors to touch the world. Our contemporary gospel has bred complacency instead of compassion, success instead of sacrifice, prestige instead of prayer. We no longer ask what we can do for Him, but rather what He can do for us. Do you see the incredible carnality of it all?

We have failed to change the world—so the world has changed us! Its methods have become our methods and we are governed by its mindset. We wear its ungodly fashions, listen to its demonic music, and watch its sensual stars. Its pollution pours into our homes and our children look anything but holy. When Christian conferences have filled hotels, pay-per-view pornography has skyrocketed. (This has happened more than once!) Do we think that God no longer sees?

The Lord has called us to be holy and set apart from sin, just as He is holy. But are we really much different than the unsaved? We have been greedy, covetous, divisive, and slanderous. We have been undisciplined in our spending, family life has become a burden, and we have made celebrities out of our leaders. Instead of producing self-effacing ministries that exalt the Lord, we have created man-centered, flesh-exalting, personality cults. Adultery and sexual sin are everywhere, and so many of us are ruled by bodily lusts. Is this the "glorious Church"?

We have put our treasures in earthly things. Heaven and hell have become figures of speech. There is hardly any brokenness for the lost. (Do we really believe people without Jesus are lost—forever?) How often have we wept for an unsaved family member or friend? And if our stomach is not our god, why so little fasting for a genuine revival and outpouring? Why so little sacrifice here if eternal life is our real goal?

Yes, God has promised to revive His people. He has promised to turn our hearts back. But before He encourages He will cleanse, and before He empowers He will purify.

Revival and restoration are at hand. But before resurrection comes death. Do we recognize how sick we are?

Chapter 2

A People in Need of the Great Physician

According to Charles Finney, "A 'Revival of Religion' presupposes a declension. It presupposes that the Church is sunk down in a backslidden state, and a revival consists in the return of the Church from her backslidings, and in the conversion of sinners."

How does backsliding set in, and what are the first steps in spiritual declension?

There is a clear lesson to be learned from the history of the children of Israel. *They served God as long as they experienced Him* (see Josh. 24:31). When His mighty works became only a memory, they gradually fell back into sin.

Moses made it clear:

It was not with our fathers that the Lord made this covenant, but with us, with all of us who are alive here today (Deut. 5:3).

Your children were not the ones who saw and experienced the discipline of the Lord your God...but it was your own eyes that saw all these great things the Lord has done (Deut. 11:2-7).

Every generation in Israel must have a personal encounter with the living God. This holds true for all peoples and nations. Grandpa's stories won't do. There is no such thing as a "second generation Pentecost." "He is not the God of the dead, but of the living" (Mt. 22:32). Are you experiencing Him today?

For many, when the acts of God become only a memory, skepticism sets in. When Elisha announced that in one day's time, a terrible famine would be turned into an abundant supply, the king's attendant replied, "Look, even if the Lord should open the floodgates of heaven, could this happen?" (2 Kings 7:2) He had heard all about the Ten Plagues, the Exodus, and Mt. Sinai. But for him it was only a story. And when the miracle of provision occurred, he saw it with his own eyes but couldn't partake of a drop (2 Kings 7:17-20).

And that is the tragedy of skepticism: it confirms itself in unbelief. The skeptic has been disappointed too many times before. He is not willing to get his hopes up again. All his childlike expectation is gone. Even if God did work miracles in the past, for the skeptic, there are none today.

Thus, skepticism soon gives way to hardened unbelief, and hardened unbelief produces rationalistic doctrines. Why else would people invent such spiritually bankrupt teachings, unless their own lives were hopelessly empty?

Would someone who was miraculously healed teach that divine healing was no more? Would an eyewitness of the Spirit's gifts and power claim that these manifestations ceased? The fact is, it is only those whose experience is devoid of the power of God who deny His power for today, since rationalistic doctrine is simply the rewriting of a supernatural Bible to suit a non-supernatural experience.

Obviously, the only thing that such doctrines can produce is religious formality, and religious formalists are revival's greatest enemies, since "they have a form of godliness, but deny its power" (2 Tim. 3:5). They hide behind a cloak of "spiritual sophistication," while in reality their hearts are coarse and hard, full of unbelief.

"But don't these people really believe the Bible, just in a different way?" How can they, when they have effectively denied the God of the Bible in terms of the here and now? Even if they claim to accept the miraculous events of the past, it is only by mental assent, since a truly living faith must have a God who is still alive.

Yes, it is possible to disagree on doctrines and differ on minor points. And, no, you don't have to be "charismatic" to be saved. But those who cynically explain away the supernatural of God may never see His power.

Sadly enough, many of those who most vehemently oppose revival are often people who once tasted the Spirit's reality. Yet through personal sin, intellectual pride, wrong teaching, or shattered hopes and dreams, they lost the zeal they once had. And when they are confronted again with the real thing, they attack those who are experiencing it, rather than humbling themselves and turning back.

It is tragic but true: revival's greatest opposers will be "religious" people who refuse to repent.

But not everyone goes the way of religious unbelief. There is another choice that people can make when their experience does not equal the message they preach. They can unconsciously exaggerate their experience and make it into something that it is not. They can say, "this is that" which the prophet proclaimed, and thus cheapen the reality of what was promised. And when we claim we're experiencing Bible days, we downgrade the days of the Bible.

This is the great indictment against our "Spirit-filled" congregations: we have had the fanfare without the fire, the hype without the happening. *With all our boasts, with all our noise, with all our big talk, we are a generation that has experienced precious little of the fullness of God.*

We must be honest with ourselves: Have we ever seen someone who was born totally blind healed in front of our eyes? Have we witnessed the instantaneous restoration of a quadriplegic? When is the last time we saw a whole community repent and be saved? Was our congregational building ever literally shaken? But that is what "Bible days" were about!

Can't we acknowledge that something is lacking when our so-called "miracle services" are anything but miraculous? Can we continue to watch the deformed cripples wheeled in and out of our meetings while people with backaches and headaches are healed? Doesn't this scene remind us of Nazareth, where Jesus could not do any miracles, "except lay His hands on a few sick people and heal them. *And*

He was amazed at their lack of faith" (Mark 6:5-6)? Isn't it time that we admit to our unbelief? If we were really in faith, things would be different!

In 1825, Charles Finney was ministering in the town of New York Mills. His brother-in-law invited him to visit the local cotton factory of which he was in charge. When Finney, who was known for his preaching in the area, entered the factory, his glance fell upon a girl who had made a jestful comment to her friend. The evangelist describes what happened next:

> When I came within eight or ten feet of her I looked solemnly at her. She observed it, and was quite overcome, and sank down and burst into tears. The impression caught almost like powder and in a few moments all in the room were in tears. The feeling spread through the factory. The owner...said to the superintendent, "Stop the mill, and let the people attend to religion; for it is more important that our souls should be saved than this factory should run."...The revival went through the mill with astonishing power and in a few days nearly all were converted.

Have we seen such a thing all our lives?

Yes, I know that God is at work today, and even now He is performing wonders all over the earth. And I know that He is restoring His glory to His people. But it is high time that we woke up to the fact that our so-called "river" is only a "puddle", and our "mighty outpouring" is barely a "trickle". Our hype will never raise the dead or even challenge our society. What our spiritual fathers experienced may have been real, but it surely isn't here today!

And when the acts of God become only a memory, watch out, because pretty soon the fear of God is gone. That is exactly where we stand today.

Chapter 3

Taken Captive by the World!

No one falls overnight. Backsliding is a gradual process. It may take a man twenty years to walk away from God. What we sow this week may not be reaped for months or even years. Blessings experienced today may be the result of yesterday's planting. What will your next harvest bring?

The prophet Isaiah declared:

When Your judgments are in the earth, the inhabitants of the world learn righteousness (Is. 26:9).

On the other hand...

where there is no [prophetic] revelation, the people cast off restraint (Prov. 29:18).

Let's face the facts: as much as we love the Lord, the fear of the Lord helps keep us from sin. The Scriptures are clear on this point:

Since you call on a Father who judges each man's work impartially, live your lives as strangers here in reverent fear...for our "God is a consuming fire" (1 Pet. 1:17; Heb. 12:29).

This is New Testament truth!

What happens when the fear of the Lord becomes only a religious cliché?

In Ezekiel chapter 8, as the prophet sits in his house with the elders of Judah before him, he is suddenly taken to Jerusalem in a vision. He is shown the abominations being committed in the Temple, and then he hears these words:

> Son of man, have you seen what the elders of the house of Israel are doing in the darkness, each at the shrine of his own idol? They say, "The Lord does not see us; the Lord has forsaken the land" (Ezek. 8:12).

One hundred and fifty years later, in Malachi's day, the problem was even worse.

> "You have said harsh things against Me," says the Lord. Yet you ask, "What have we said against you?" You have said, "It is futile to serve God. What did we gain by carrying out His requirements and going about like mourners before the Lord Almighty? But now we call the arrogant blessed. Certainly the evildoers prosper, and even those who challenge God escape. Where is the God of justice?" (Mal. 3:13-15; 2:17)

Yes, where is the God of justice? How can He let our sins multiply without intervening now? But that is the frightening thing—the sins of some men "trail behind" (1 Tim. 5:24); they are not judged immediately. The "iniquity of the Amorites" must reach its full measure (Gen. 15:16). And then the judgment will come. True, our sins will always find us out (Num. 32:23); but for some it may come too late. By the time their sins catch up with them, they will already have wasted their lives.

Consider again the history of Israel. God ordered his people to utterly destroy the Canaanites. His command was simple and clear: Annihilate and exterminate! Yet Israel did not take His words seriously. They did not see the sinfulness of sin. They failed to see that the Canaanites could kill.

So they left a remnant of the nations scattered throughout their land, and those that survived became thorns in their sides. Israel was constantly harassed by peoples that should not have been alive, yet now they had no strength to resist them.

And then a strange thing happened. The Canaanites became their friends. "They're not so bad after all! Maybe there *is* something to their religious practices; they're certainly more fun than ours! Moses was probably afraid we'd find out—that's why he told us to destroy them. And to think! If I had listened to that narrow minded Yahweh doctrine I would have ended up killing my daughter-in-law! Now we're just one happy family!"

And then something tragic happened. The Canaanites became their masters, "for a man is a slave to whatever has mastered him" (2 Pet. 2:19). Having given themselves to the lusts of the flesh, they soon found themselves ruled by them. And then they cried out to the Lord. But for that lost generation, it was too late.

We must learn the lesson from Israel's past. We must take God's Word seriously. Sin kills. The world pollutes. Following the flesh means death.

A fifteen year old girl from Long Island fell into rebellion against her parents. She left home and hitchhiked out of state. A trucker picked her up and paid her to commit a sexual act. Afterwards she wept in shame. But the guilt quickly disappeared. Within a few months of her arrival in Texas she had fallen into prostitution.

Soon she became so popular and made so much money that the other prostitutes began to turn on her. She decided to flee while she had the chance, but she was caught by the pimp and his wife. When her naked corpse was pulled out of the river, a police chief said that it was the most brutally tortured body he had ever seen. She had cigarette burns from head to toe, her jaw was broken, and she was shot through the mouth. The devil is playing for keeps.

There is only one way to deal with Satan and his fallen ways (Deut. 7:2-5): *Make no treaty with him and show him no mercy.* We can not compromise with the world! A little leaven leavens the whole lump. *Do not intermarry with the devil's people.* Marrying or even dating the unsaved is out! It violates our covenant with God. *Do not worship this world's idols.* We can not be enamored by sinful and immoral stars! Their life-styles and fashions are not for us. *Do not covet his silver or gold.* We can not consume our lives pursuing material wealth! Selling out to the Lord means turning our backs on carnal desires.

> *Do not bring a detestable thing into your house or you, like it, will be set apart for destruction. Utterly abhor and detest it, for it is set apart for destruction* (Deut. 7:25-26).

We can not bring ungodly movies, books, and magazines into our homes and expect to be exempt from the judgment of God.

Strong words, yes, and hard on the flesh. But if we do not destroy sin, sin will destroy us. If we do not subdue the flesh, the flesh will subdue us.

Remember King Saul.

It was the Amalekites that he failed to wipe out (1 Sam. 15).

It was an Amalekite that put him to death (2 Sam. 1).

Chapter 4

Prerequisites for Revival

Our only hope of breaking out of this sinful cycle is revival. And if we are going to have revival, then we are going to have to become hungry. Hungry for God and hungry for souls. In fact, we are going to have to be starving. The time of desperation must come when we are so consumed with a passion for revival that we can hardly eat, drink, or sleep without longing for it. Then we are on the right track.

How do we start? First, like Gideon, we must challenge our present state and acknowledge our lack.

Try and picture the scene. There is Gideon, threshing wheat in a winepress for fear of the Midianites, when the angel of the Lord addresses him, "The Lord is with you, mighty warrior!"

"The Lord is with me? Mighty warrior?"

Who are you kidding? My nation is oppressed by foreigners, I'm hiding here in a closet, and we can't even lift up our heads! "If the Lord is really with us, why has all this happened to us? Where are all His wonders that our fathers told us about, saying 'Surely the Lord delivered us out of Egypt?' "

To this the angel replied:

Go in this strength of yours and deliver Israel out of the hand of Midian. I am surely sending you (Judg. 6:12-14).

What was Gideon's strength? It was the realization that if God was truly with His people things would be different. Do you see that? This is the first step toward revival and freedom: the recognition of the fact that if the Bible is true, if the promises of God are real, if His miracles are not merely old myths, things should be different.

Thank God there are Gideon's today who are also raising their voices; men and women who are sick of hearing stories about "the good old days" and promises of "the coming great revival"; men and women who know deep within that there must be something more, who have had it with singing about the glory without ever experiencing it; men and women who see with total clarity that the Church is not living as if Jesus is Lord.

Look at our American scene today. The reproach we suffer is not for the Messiah's sake; we are not scorned because of our militant stand. No. We are mocked because of our leaders' sins, because of our failure to be holy and clean. Gospel and greed seem to go hand in hand, and our society equates evangelist with exploiter. Yet Jesus is the Head of the Body! How can this be?

The world is unreached, tens of thousands die daily, and Islam and the cults march on. Yet we waste away our lives before our big screen TVs, claiming our blessings *in Him*. And all the while Jesus, the Savior of the World, pours out His heart *in us*: "I gave My blood for the people of this world. I gave My life for theirs. Won't you go reach them with My love? I have no other voice than yours." Do you hear His urgent pleading?

The road to revival begins with confession, with a heartfelt admission of poverty and need. It begins with contrition, with fasting and groaning, with the proud in heart forced to their knees. And it begins with a purging, a "spirit of burning"; it begins with the call to repent.

Chapter 5

The Lost Art of Repentance

The Hebrew word for repent means "to turn" or "turn back." Over and over the prophets proclaimed, "Turn back to God and He will turn back to you!" Turn away from your sins and turn back to God, and He will turn away from His anger and turn back to you. Or, *when Israel repents, God relents*.

But repentance was not only the theme of the Hebrew prophets. It was the foundation of Jesus' own message ("The Kingdom of God is near. *Repent* and believe the good news!" "Unless you *repent*, you too will all perish.") and the heart of the great commission ("*Repentance* and forgiveness of sins must be preached to all nations, beginning at Jerusalem.") It was the key to Peter's preaching ("*Repent* and be baptized, every one of you!") and the essence of Paul's gospel ("God calls all men everywhere to *repent*.") Without repentance and faith, no one can be saved.

Repentance means spiritual revolution. Strongholds of sin are demolished. Lifetime bondages are overcome. Hardened hearts break open. Satan's grip is undone. Repentance sets the prisoners free!

Yet many of our leaders have taught, "You can have Jesus as Savior without having Him as Lord. Jesus already died for your sins, so don't even think about that junk. Just confess Him with your lips, believe in your heart, and it's done!" In other words,"You can believe today and repent tomorrow!" But does tomorrow ever come? Is this how people got saved in the Bible? Does it even make spiritual sense?

Actually, this no-repentance gospel hardly resembles the message of the Scriptures, since according to the Word: 1) There is no forgiveness where there is no repentance (Acts 3:19); 2) You can no more believe without repenting than you can repent without believing (How can you believe in God without turning back to Him? And how can you turn back to God without believing in Him?); and 3) It is impossible to come to God without repenting, since repentance is the very act of coming back. For those taken captive by the devil, repentance is the only way out (2 Tim. 2:25-26).

What kind of fruit has this "salvation without sacrifice" message produced? It has brought about a whole generation of double-minded "believers," a multitude of worldly "children of God." It has filled our church buildings without changing men's hearts. But a great shaking is coming to the Body. And while the "no-cross gospel" has drawn the big crowds, the numbers will not stand when the shaking arrives.

But what about repentance for those already saved? Do believers need to repent? Haven't we become the righteousness of God in the Messiah? Aren't we new creations in Him? Or, to paraphrase what you're likely to hear when you talk to believers about repentance, "Quit preaching condemnation! I'm free from all that stuff. I repented when I got saved."

But did they truly repent when they got saved? Were they really challenged to "count the cost"? Have they genuinely "taken up the cross" and followed Jesus? Are they dead to sin and alive to God? And today, where are their lives? What have they done since they've been born again?

Unfortunately, many of those who stumble over the repentance message *now that they are in the church* are the very ones who never heard it *when they were in the world.* We've told the lost, "You don't have to give up anything! Just add Jesus to your life and do your thing for Him!" Then we tell the saved, "You've arrived, you're complete! The past is all dead. Keep doing your thing for Him!"

But where is the message of repentance? Where is the preaching of the cross? As believers, how often have we been challenged to "examine ourselves" and "test ourselves" (2 Cor. 13:5)? Have we forgotten that we must "judge ourselves" if we do not want to be judged with the world (1 Cor. 11:31-32)? Doesn't the Word tell us plainly that we must "purify ourselves from everything that contaminates body and spirit, perfecting holiness out of reverence for God" (2 Cor. 7:1)? Isn't this why there are thousands of selfish, superficial, and shallow believers with only skin deep professions, because they have never been called to repent?

Yet this so-called "Good News" not only hurts those who hear it. *It degrades the very sacrifice of the Messiah and demeans the blood of Jesus.* It implies that the Son of God has little claim on our lives and that He does not deserve our all. It suggests that our sin was not so bad and that we were not under the judgment of God. And when we "make deals" with people to sell them our faith ("Just look at all the good things God will give you if you follow Him!") we forget that *the Lord Himself* is the great prize of our salvation, and that eternal life means knowing Him.

Does the Church need to repent? Is this message still for our day? Let's see what Jesus has to say!

> To the angel of the CHURCH of Ephesus write: ...I hold this against you: You have forsaken your first love. Remember the height from which you have fallen! REPENT and do the things you did at first. If you do not REPENT, I will come to you and remove your lampstand from its place (Rev. 2:1,5).

> To the angel of the CHURCH of Pergamum write: ...I have a few things against you. You have people there who hold to the teaching of Balaam...[and] you also have those who hold to the teaching of the Nicolaitans. REPENT therefore! Otherwise, I will soon come to you and will fight against them with the sword of My mouth (Rev. 2:12,14-16).

> To the angel of the CHURCH in Thyatira write: ...I have this against you: You tolerate that woman Jezebel, who calls herself a prophetess...I have given her time to REPENT of her immorality, but she is unwilling. So I will cast her on a

bed of suffering and I will make those who commit adultery with her suffer intensely, unless they REPENT of their ways (Rev. 2:18,20-22).

To the angel of the CHURCH in Sardis write: …I know your deeds; you have a reputation of being alive, but you are dead. Wake up! Strengthen what remains and is about to die, for I have not found your deeds complete in the sight of My God. Remember, therefore, what you have received and heard; obey it and REPENT (Rev. 3:1-3).

To the angel of the CHURCH in Laodicea write: …I know your deeds, that you are neither hot nor cold. I wish you were either one or the other! So, because you are lukewarm—neither hot nor cold—I am about to spew you out of My mouth…Those whom I love I rebuke and discipline. So be earnest, and REPENT (Rev. 3:14-16,19).

Are we getting the message loud and clear? We must turn back to God if we've turned away. His grace flows out towards those who repent.

Chapter 6

Repentance Prepares the Way

The preaching of repentance prepares the way of the Lord. Yet "repent" is one of the most unpopular words in the religious dictionary. It is challenging, unnerving, and intimidating. It accuses of guilt and calls for a change. It implies that all is not well. In fact, it *proclaims* that God is not pleased.

No wonder Joseph Parker could say, "The man whose little sermon is 'repent' sets himself against his age, and will for the time being be battered mercilessly by the age whose moral tone he challenges. There is but one end for such a man—'off with his head!' You had better not try to preach repentance until you have pledged your head to heaven."

Without repentance there can be no revival, for "the depth of any revival will be determined exactly by the spirit of repentance that is obtained. In fact, this is the *key* to every true revival born of God" (Frank Bartleman). So if you want revival, you must have repentance; if you want God to come, you must prepare His way.

Consider the ministry of John the Baptist. Do you think he "pledged his head to heaven"? John came as the "voice of one calling out in the desert, '*Prepare the way of the Lord*, make straight paths for Him.' " His message was simple and blunt: "*Repent*, for the kingdom of heaven is near." His baptism was straight to the point: "I baptize with water for *repentance*." And he minced no words with the crowds: "Produce fruit in keeping with *repentance*" (Mt. 3:1-11). He cleared out the sin and made room for the King by preaching his sermon, "Repent!"

How does the preaching of repentance prepare the way of the Lord?

1) *The preaching of repentance prepares the way of the Lord by humbling the proud.* Before this word every "mountain and hill" are "made low" (Is. 40:4). It pronounces all men guilty before the righteous Judge, and it strips them of their arrogance, telling them they are nothing, and bringing them to their knees. Who can be proud when measured against the standards of God?

> For the Lord Almighty has a day in store for all the proud and lofty, for all that is exalted (and they will be humbled) (Is. 2:12).

When men bow down with their faces to the ground, God is ready to come!

2) *The preaching of repentance prepares the way of the Lord by exposing man-made religion.* The essence of all man-made religion is simply this: while claiming to fulfill

the commandments of God, it actually makes them void. By exalting the sacred traditions of men, it nullifies the word of God. It sets itself up in the place of God. Thus, *all man-made religion is idolatry*, since idolatry is simply bowing down to the work of man's hands. Do you see how idolatry dominates many a church in our land?

We bow down to *our* systems, *our* goals, and *our* plans; the will of the people often dethrones the will of God. Fleshly bureaucrats run many a committee, and human politics govern and rule. Many are building their kingdom, not His. Can we really say, "Jesus is Lord"?

The message of repentance smashes all idols. It calls for unqualified submission to the absolute will of God. It demands that all foreign gods be removed and destroyed. It does not tolerate the presence of any other ruling force. It makes room for the One Rightful King.

3) *The preaching of repentance prepares the way of the Lord by removing the presence of willful and chronic sin.* Before God will come to bless, sin must be removed. Otherwise, His coming spells destruction. This is the heartbeat of the call to repent: "Get rid of everything unclean! Prepare to meet your God. He is holy and He is coming your way." (Mark this down: When repentance is being preached in the power of the Spirit, not in a condemning, hopeless way, but with a dynamic, life-giving anointing, divine visitation is near!)

Are we ready today for the coming of God? Not with so much habitual sin! In fact, the only way that the American Church will experience a glorious visitation is if believers start "kicking their habits." Otherwise His visitation will be anything but "glorious." Are we slaves to cigarettes or television or lust or overeating or money or gossip? All addictions must go!

Let's face the facts: We can not serve two masters. Every time we sin we personally offend God. Sin is disloyalty to Jesus. Sin grieves the Holy Spirit. He hates its very stain with a passion. Its scent is an ugly stink. It excludes the presence of the Lord. Will God really come to a sin-plagued Church? Only to say: repent!

Stop for a moment and ask yourself a question: Do you sincerely want God in your life? (Think twice before you answer!) Then all known sin must be removed and all ungodliness abandoned. Now is the time to come clean.

4) *The preaching of repentance prepares the way of the Lord by lifting up the humble broken-hearted ones.* Before God comes, "every valley" must be "lifted up." The "little ones" must have their place. The poor in spirit must be blessed. The meek must have their day.

Repentance is the great equalizer. It shuts us all up to the mercy of God. It removes all man-made distinctions. It restores true Kingdom order. It makes the last first and the first last. It esteems the humble in heart. It exalts those who honor the Lord.

While the winds of repentance batter the proud, they are a breath of fresh air to the broken-hearted. "The nearer I get to God, the more broken I am in spirit" (Smith Wigglesworth). "Blessed are the poor in spirit, for theirs is the kingdom of heaven" (Mt. 5:3).

These are the ones with whom He will dwell, "to revive the spirit of the lowly and to revive the heart of the contrite" (Is. 57:15). These are the ones He will exalt.

God found a contrite young man in Wales in 1904. While preparing himself for the ministry, this 26 year old coal miner heard an evangelist pray, "Lord, do this, and this, and this, etc., and bend us." The words "bend us" became etched on his mind. Soon after he became consumed.

> I fell on my knees with my arms over the seat in front of me, my face bathed in perspiration, and the tears flowing in streams, so that I thought it must be blood gushing forth...For about two minutes it was terrible. I cried out, "Bend me! Bend me! Bend us! Oh! Oh! Oh! Oh!"

What was it that bent him so?

> "It was God's commending His love which bent me, while I saw nothing in it to commend."

He was bent by amazing grace!

> "Then the fearful bending of the judgment day came to my mind, and I was filled with compassion for those who must bend at the judgment, and I wept."

Evan Roberts continued to pray, "Bend the church, save the world." In less than six months, over 100,000 were saved.

Bend *us* today, oh Lord!

Chapter 7

The Time for Revival Has Come

Our country needs a revival. We have gone more than two entire generations without a nation-wide move of God. We are running on less than empty, on the dregs instead of the fuel. *A time of refreshing must come.*

We have seen pockets of limited blessing and showers of minor effect. We have seen biblical truths restored and spiritual gifts recovered. But what about a coast to coast awakening? What about a national shaking? What about *revival* in our land?

What makes revival different than normal patterns of church growth? What are the traits of a real visitation?

A true revival is absolutely supernatural in its working. It is totally God-glorifying in its character. No flesh can boast in its presence. It can not be produced, manufactured, or worked up. It is poured out, poured on, and poured in, a deluge of God from heaven. It carries all things along on the crest of its waves; it is driven by the wind of the Spirit.

Listen to one observer's report of the Welsh Revival of 1904:

There is something there from the other world. You can not say whence it came or whither it is going, but it moves and lives and reaches for you all the time. You see men and women go down in sobbing agony before your eyes as the invisible Hand clutches your heart. And you shudder (William T. Stead).

Revival comes from God!

A true revival is sudden and spontaneous. It can not be orchestrated or scheduled. You can not "fit it in." It can not be thought out or planned for. It frustrates methods of man. Revival bursts forth like a torrent. No one is ready for the flood—even when you know it's coming!

When the day of Pentecost came, they were all together in one place. Suddenly a sound like the blowing of a violent wind came from heaven and filled the whole house where they were sitting. They saw what seemed to be tongues of fire that separated and came to rest on each of them. All of them were filled with the Holy Spirit and began to speak in other tongues as the Spirit enabled them (Acts 2:1-4).

Have you ever thought back to that day? If any group of believers was ever prepared, it was that group of 120. Yet the Spirit still came *suddenly* with a sound like the blowing of a *violent* wind. It was the first day of a great biblical feast, but His coming was still a surprise. The disciples had no idea what they were in for. So it is with every genuine move of God. It is always more than you expect!

A true revival is uncontrollable and uncontainable. No human agency can rule it; no group can hem it in. No church can set its limits; it spreads like wild fire. All you can do is get out of the way! Can you reason with a tornado or argue with a tidal wave? Can you harness the power of a hurricane or control the force of an earthquake? How much less can you contain the Spirit of God? When God's glory comes, human efforts must cease.

> The cloud covered the Tent of Meeting, and the glory of the Lord filled the tabernacle. Moses could not enter the Tent of Meeting because the glory of the Lord filled the tabernacle (Ex. 40:34-35).

> The temple of the Lord was filled with a cloud, and the priests could not perform their service because of the cloud, for the glory of the Lord filled the temple of God (2 Chron. 5:13-14).

God's presence excludes all performance.

A true revival brings an overwhelming revelation of the holiness of God and the sinfulness of man. In revival, God reveals Himself as He really is. The blinders are taken off our eyes. Trite religious cliches fall aside. You are given a vision of God.

Do you realize that God is so holy that just *seeing* Him convicts you of sin? Those who are closest to His throne are overwhelmed.

> They never stop saying, Holy, holy, holy is the Lord God Almighty, who was, and is, and is to come...the twenty-four elders fall down before Him who sits on the throne, and worship Him who lives for ever and ever. They lay their crowns before the throne and say, "You are worthy, our Lord and God" (Rev. 4:8-11).

Our God is so awesome and pure!

Isaiah was a prophet. Yet when he saw the Lord he was completely undone:

> Woe to me! I am ruined! For I am a man of unclean lips, and
> I live among a people of unclean lips, and my eyes have seen
> the King, the Lord Almighty! (Is. 6:5)

Job was a righteous man commended by God. Yet in
light of God's splendor he was only a worm:

> My ears had heard of You but now my eyes have seen You.
> Therefore I despise myself and repent in dust and ashes (Job
> 42:5-6).

Simon Peter went fishing with Jesus. He let the Master
teach out of his boat. But when the might and power of the
Lord were revealed, "he fell at Jesus' knees and said, 'Go
away from me Lord; I am a sinful man' " (Lk. 5:8).

*The best cure for a self-righteous spirit is an open vision
of God.* Revival reveals God. His people weep and repent.
The unsaved groan in their sins. Then mercy is poured out.

A true revival transforms those it touches. People are
genuinely saved. Hardened sinners snap in two. Chronic
backsliders are delivered. Shallow believers dive deep. One
moment of divine visitation bears more fruit than twenty
years of counseling and teaching. God confirms His word.

"We had all heard our fathers speak of the great effects
which they in their youth had seen accompanying the
preaching of the word, and the influence which the outpouring of the spirit was wont to have on the minds of the
people assembled for worship; but we had never seen the
like ourselves, at least in the measure which our fathers
were accustomed to say they had seen; and, therefore, a
kind of scepticism concerning its reality frequently possessed us. But now this scepticism was to be taken away

for ever" (From the Welsh Revival of 1859). Revival brings lasting results.

A true revival has a life giving effect on the society as a whole. It does not just take place "in the church." It is not confined to a building. It flows out and changes the world. Several factors bring this about.

First, when large numbers of sinners get saved, there is not so much sinning going on! Less murderers means lower murder rates. A decrease in thieves means a decline in theft. When drug dealers get delivered, drug dealing diminishes. In times of revival, bars are converted to churches, and pornographic theaters are used for evangelistic rallies. The owners have gotten saved!

This is not the only factor that impacts the society. God's people have come alive too! They are actively standing for righteousness. They are confronting sin on their jobs and ungodliness in their communities. Their lives have become truly holy. They shine forth God's light like a torch. Justice returns to the courts. Reverence returns to the schools. Jesus is Lord of His Church!

But there is one more spiritual influence, an unseen power at work. There is a supernatural "chain reaction," a "divine radiation zone" (Winkie Pratney). The angels of God are everywhere. The armies of heaven have come. The very air is filled with God's presence. Conviction pervades the atmosphere. Dreadful fear grips the godless.

Here is a typical account: In Coleraine, Ireland, in 1859, revival had reached fever pitch. When a school boy testified in class of his great joy in finding the Lord, the Spirit began to move on the other students.

> Boy after boy rose and silently left the room. When the master investigated what was happening to his class he found these boys ranged alongside the wall of the play-ground, everyone apart on his knees! Their silent prayer soon became a bitter cry which brought conviction to those inside—not only the other boys, but to the girls' schoolroom above. Soon the whole school was on its knees, and its wail of distress brought people flocking in from the street who, as they crossed the threshold, came under the same convict-ing power. Every room was filled with men, women, and children seeking God (Arthur Wallis).

Examples like this could be quoted almost without limit. *Heaven-sent revivals are real!*

Can you see now where our so-called revivals of recent years have fallen short? Can you see how superficial they were? Do you realize where they have been lacking? Do you see how bankrupt we are?

If we can see this, we are moving in the right direction. *It is only the hungry that He fills.*

Chapter 8

One Nation Under God— The Key to America's Greatness

America has been indelibly marked by its revivals. The significant outpourings of the Spirit which occurred here over the last three hundred years have deeply altered our history. Every major, positive, national change in our society can be traced back to the influence of revival, and *our steady moral decline in the 20th century is a direct result of the absence of any large scale revival.*

Many American believers today are almost totally unaware of the powerful movings of God which swept through this land in the 18th and 19th centuries. Let me put you in remembrance:

1741—Enfield, New England. It was here that one of the most remarkable revivals took place. God had begun to stir the New England area out of its worldliness, apathy and unbelief in the mid 1730's. But the town of Enfield remained untouched. Jonathan Edwards, the brilliant philosopher, theologian and, shortly before his death, president of Princeton University, was scheduled to preach there one Sunday. (We would hardly call it preaching today! He *read* his text *monotone and without gestures,* and because his eyesight was so poor, he held the pages pressed up to his face!) The congregation was a casual, godless bunch. But the neighboring town had been in deep travail the previous night for God to extend His mercy on that group.

On that Sunday, July 8th of 1741, as Edwards read his famous message, "Sinners in the Hands of an Angry God," something extraordinary began to occur. The fear of God fell. The congregants began to see themselves as hopelessly lost, dangling by a thread over the jumping fires of hell. (It was a vivid sermon!) Soon there was so much screaming, crying out, and fainting that Edwards had to order them to be quiet so that his message could be heard. *People began unconsciously to cling to their pews and grasp hold of the pillars of the church so as not to slip into hell.* These were the days of the First Great Awakening in our land!

From 1740-1745, *300,000 souls* were added to the Kingdom. (There were only 2,000,000 people in the American colonies at that time!) Before the revival, young people caroused and partied all night. In the height of this time of awakening, which had been greatly aided by the ministry of George Whitefield from England and had reached to the American Indians through the prevailing prayer of David Brainerd, even Benjamin Franklin could say that "it seemed as if all the world were growing religious, so that one could not walk through the town in the evening without hearing psalms sung in different families of every street."

1801—Cane Ridge, on the Western Frontier. An astounding 20,000 people from the sparsely populated frontier regions had gathered together for a special six-day outdoor camp meeting. The crowds were addressed by many different preachers from varying denominations, using fallen logs and the like for their pulpits. Here are some eye-witness reports:

"I stepped up on a log where I could have a better view of the surging sea of humanity. The scene that then presented itself to my mind was indescribable. At once I saw at least five hundred swept down in a moment as if a battery of a thousand guns had been opened upon them and then immediately followed shrieks and shouts that rent the very heavens."

"On Sabbath [Sunday] night I saw above one hundred candles burning at once—and I saw, I suppose, one hundred persons of all ages from eight to sixty years at once on the ground crying for mercy...The sensible, the weak, learned and unlearned, the rich and the poor are the subjects of it."

The Wild West was being tamed, and the wilderness being revived. *The whole region underwent a deep moral transformation.* The Spirit of God had come.

1857—New York City. It was here that the great Prayer Revival took root. The churches at that time were becoming worldly and internalized, and immorality, violent crime, spiritualism, corruption and atheism were on the rise (J. Edwin Orr).

Does this have a familiar sound?

Jeremiah Lanphier, a retired businessman become missionary, acting in obedience to the Spirit's prompting, began to promote a weekly "Lunch Hour Prayer Meeting" for revival. Only six attended the first meeting, and twenty the second. But within several months, tens of thousands were praying seven days a week, around the clock! The revival spread from city to city, jumped across the ocean to

England, Ireland and Wales, and shaped the history of our nation.

> From 1857-1858 in America alone, over 1,000,000 non-church members were born again, in addition to about 1,000,000 formerly unsaved church members. *At the height of the revival there were over 50,000 new births a week.* As a result of this revival hitting Chicago, the 40 year ministry of D. L. Moody was born. And within a decade, slavery was legally abolished.

> The Revival of 1857 restored integrity to government and business in America once again. There was renewed obedience to the social commandments. An intense sympathy was created for the poor and needy. A compassionate society was rebirthed. The reins of America were returned to the godly. Yet another time, Revival became the solution to the problems, the remedy for the evils, the cure of all ills (Mary Stuart Relfe).

Then in 1906 in California, the fire fell at Azusa Street. From there, the flames of the 20th century Pentecostal renewal began to spread across the globe.

Our country has been in sin before. There have been times of immorality and drunkenness on the streets, skepticism and atheism on college campuses, and coldness and worldliness in the churches. The gospel has been totally mocked and dismissed as outdated many times in the past. *Revival turned things around then. Revival will do it again.*

Chapter 9

Restoring the Truth of God

Revival comes when things are wrong. It comes to set them right. It renews and corrects and fixes and repairs. It comes to make us whole.

Jesus never needed to be revived during His earthly life and ministry. He brought revival with Him! He was a walking revival! He was never out of His Father's will. He never grew cold. He never fell. He never left His Father's side. His love never wavered or waned.

The One who sent Me is with Me; He has not left Me alone, for I always do what pleases Him (Jn. 8:29).

The principle is the same with us. *If we continually walked and lived in the presence of God, we would never need revival.* But that is not the case. We often get dragged down with the cares of this world. We neglect certain aspects of the Word, both in practice and in doctrine. We easily get off track without even knowing it. Without great diligence, we drift.

Revival comes to turn us back, to restore our lives in God. It shakes us and wakes us and lifts us up. It tells us, "You are off!"—and then turns us on.

Where are we off today? What does God want to restore?

1) *Revival restores Jesus to His rightful position as the Head of the Body.* This is God's central purpose, His number one priority. Paul expresses it clearly:

> [Jesus] is the image of the invisible God, the firstborn over all creation... All things were created by Him and for Him. He is before all things, and in Him all things hold together. And He is the head of the body, the church; He is the beginning and the firstborn from the dead, so that in everything He might have the supremacy (Col. 1:15-18).

Who is exalted "to the highest place" (Phil. 2:9),

> far above all rule and authority, power and dominion, and every title that can be given, not only in the present age but also in the one to come" (Eph. 1:21)?

JESUS! At *His* name, every knee will bow,

> in heaven and on earth and under the earth, and every tongue [will] confess that Jesus Christ is Lord to the glory of God the Father (Phil. 2:10).

Jesus must come first!

Now consider for a moment that God is a Jealous God. When He revealed Himself to Moses He told him that His very name was "Jealous" (Ex. 34). Can you begin to imagine just how jealous the Heavenly Father is for His own Son?—His Son who bled, and agonized, and took our sins?—His Son who died a criminal's death just so that we

could be saved?—His Son who shared His glory before the
world began, and in whom all the Father's fulness dwells?
Can you understand how deeply God feels for His Son?

This is why,

> Revival, above everything else, is a glorification of the
> Lord Jesus Christ, the Son of God. It is the restoration of
> him to the centre of the life of the Church...It leads to our
> hymns, our anthems of praise: Christ the centre of the
> Church (D. Martyn Lloyd-Jones).

Do you understand this now?

God is fighting for His Son. He is reminding us how
much we owe the Lamb. He is showing us again how wonderful Jesus is. During times of revival, people have been
caught up for hours in a holy presence, meditating on the
love of Jesus.

> The heart was swallowed up in a kind of glow of Christ's
> love coming down as a constant stream of sweet light, at the
> same time the soul all flowing out in love to Him; so that
> there seemed to be a constant flowing and reflowing from
> heart to heart (Jonathan Edwards).

Loving the Lord with all our hearts! *That* is the meaning
of life.

In a revived church, Jesus reigns supreme. He is preached
about, sung about, worshiped, and praised. The cross and
the blood become central themes. That is where the great
price was paid. That is the truth God will anoint, the subject
He will inspire. And that is a measuring rod from heaven:
How do we line up?

Look on the shelves of our Christian bookstores: lots of new books on lots of good subjects—but how many emphasize the cross? Listen to the latest choruses: plenty of edifying Scripture songs, but how many lyrics on the blood?

And what about our own hearts and lives? Have we taken our eyes off Jesus and put them on something else—like the gifts of the Spirit or confession or intercession or praise? Is Jesus our best and closest friend, or has He become the means through which we can attain our spiritual goals? Are we seeking *Him* or are we seeking *it*?

Revival points us back to the Door. He is still the only Way.

2) *Revival restores the fear of God.* The power of God becomes more than a charismatic expression. The judgment of God becomes more than a distant future image. The anger of God becomes more than an obsolete religious concept. In revival, God's power is here, God's judgment is now, and God's anger is real! He will not tolerate willful sin. He will not overlook mocking and slander. He will not smile at blasphemous pride. The real God appears.

His love abounds, His mercy flows, His compassion knows no end. But much is given and much is required. Responsibility comes with revival! No one can say, "I didn't know! I never saw! I never met the Lord!" No one can claim, "He wasn't there. How could I know His name?"

> The voice of the Lord strikes with flashes of lightning. The voice of the Lord shakes the desert; the Lord shakes the desert of Kadesh. The voice of the Lord twists the oaks and

strips the forest bare. And in His temple all cry, Glory! (Ps. 29:7-9)

That is the sound of revival! The Spirit comes. The Lion roars. Who can but tremble with fear?

3) *Revival restores the reality of heaven and hell.* There is no possible way that we would live as we do if our eyes were truly open to eternity. We would not be at home in this world. Our lives would be caught up with "forever." The hope of future glory would move us to sacrificial living; the sobering fact of hell would ignite our burden for the lost. Yet we sit here asleep in the light!

Here is an overwhelming truth. Every human being will experience either eternal life or eternal loss; eternal peace or eternal punishment; eternal blessing or eternal burning. There is no other choice!

Revival opens our eyes. The scales abruptly fall off. Our vision is suddenly clear. Stark truths jostle our minds. *One life, one chance, one race. One path, one truth, one place.* Eternal choices surround us. The reality staggers the soul.

You will stand before God one day; no one will hold your hand. There will be no where to hide on that day; you will have to look God in the eye. Your every thought will be revealed; your every deed reviewed. *You* will get credit or you will get blame. What will the verdict be?

Stop and think for a moment. *You could spend eternity with God.* No more sorrow, no more struggle; no more Satan, no more sin. Depression will be a thing long forgotten.

Hopelessness will forever depart. Sickness will afflict no more. God's servants will serve Him and see His face (Rev. 22:3-4). His endless joys will be there. True fulfillment will be yours—forever.

> *Be assured, the highest thoughts of man fail to approach the reality and the delights of that heavenly scene* (Marietta Davis, relating her experience of heaven in August of 1848).

Revival brings heaven near!

If we really believed this we would be changed. We would not be so carnal, so enamored by temporal things. We would not love the world. Our hearts would be in heavenly treasures (Mt. 6:19-21). Out thoughts would be "above" (Col. 3:1-3). We would be finished with the rat race of materialism and greed. We would live every day for the Lord.

But what about hell? Can there be such a place? Do we believe in an endless death? Can we relate to the concept of infinite suffering, of darkness, damnation and doom? Our thoughts and our actions, our prayers and our lives, make this fact painfully clear: *we do not believe in the existence of hell.* We have put it right out of our minds.

What happened to Evan Roberts when he saw multitudes of lost souls entering the everlasting pit?

> From sheer anguish of soul at the sight of this fearfully solemn tragedy enacted before him, he cried with fierce intensity upon God to rescue them. He pleaded that hell's door should be closed for one year so that they might have an opportunity to repent (Elfion Evans).

Could there be any other reaction? *A one minute visit to hell would change our lives for eternity.*

But are we *now* telling people the truth? Do we warn them of the judgment to come? Do we tell them of the day when people will cry out to the mountains and the rocks,

> Fall on us and hide us from the face of Him who sits on the throne and from the wrath of the Lamb (Rev. 6:16)?

Do we preach about the Jesus who "treads the winepress of the fury of the wrath of God Almighty" (Rev. 19:15)?

> Then I saw a great white throne and Him who was seated on it. Earth and sky fled from His presence, and there was no place for them. And I saw the dead, great and small, standing before the throne, and books were opened. Another book was opened, which is the book of life. The dead were judged according to what they had done as recorded in the books. If anyone's name was not found written in the book of life, he was thrown into the lake of fire (Rev. 20:11-12,15).

May God help us to see!

If we had a revelation of never ending darkness and separation from God, we would share our faith at any cost. We would fast and groan for those who didn't know the Lord. We would go to the ends of the earth just to reach our worst enemy. We would understand why Jesus went to the cross. *And we would follow Him.*

Revival comes and rocks our boat. It says to us, "This is all real!" It opens our ears to the cries of the damned. It breaks our dull hearts in two. It jolts us back to the basics in God. It is heaven's final appeal.

What does revival mean for the child of God? How does it translate into our regular daily routine? *Revival means living every hour as if Jesus were really Lord and His Word were really true.*

Chapter 10

Don't Put Out the Spirit's Fire!

How would history read if no one ever quenched the Spirit? How many worldwide awakenings would have taken place this century if church people had not stood in the way of God? What could happen in our own lives if we determined to let the Spirit move, regardless of the consequences?

Very few revivals have ever finished their God-appointed course. Very few outpourings of the Spirit have ever reached their potential. Man is always getting in the way!

There are *programs* and *plans* that must be accomplished—as if we could do God's work better than He could! The dignity of the church must be maintained—as if a visitation from heaven would be an embarrassing thing! We must keep our reputation at any price—even if it means compromise with the Lord.

What are the five words that have stopped thousands of moves of God? "The show must go on!" What a shame! Believers fast and pray for years; they cry out to God for months on end: "Revive us, refresh us, oh Lord!" And then when He comes they reject Him. He didn't fit into their plans.

Remember this: if the "front door" of the Church had been open, God would not have come through the back! If everything was right, He would not have had to rearrange! The little children praised Jesus because the others were too stiff and proud (Mt. 21:14-16). And the Son of God was born in a stable because there was no room in the inn. *Nothing has changed today.*

The Azusa outpouring took place in a run-down, renovated barn. The "leader," Daddy Seymour, sat during the meetings with his head hidden behind two boxes. Frank Bartleman wrote of this time, "Evidently the Lord had found the little company at last, outside as always, through whom He could have His way. God had not chosen an established mission where this could be done. They were in the hands of men; the Spirit could not work. Others far more pretentious had failed. That which man esteems had been passed by once more, and the Spirit born again in a humble 'stable' outside ecclesiastical establishments."

God often moves through homely and unlikely vessels to show us that *we* do not have it all. Have you ever noticed our slogans? The Baptists teach "the *whole counsel* of God" while the Pentecostals preach "the *full gospel*." The Jesus only people preach "the *apostolic doctrine*" while the Faith camp teaches "*the* Word." And the Restorationists have a "*New Testament* church." *Our* group has it all!

When David fled from Absalom, the priests accompanied him with the ark of the Lord. But David said to Zadok the priest:

> Take the ark of God back into the city. If I find favor in the Lord's eyes He will bring me back and let me see it and His dwelling place again (2 Sam. 15:25).

Do you get the point? *No man owns the ark.* The ark belongs to God. No man or group or denomination can possess it. It is for God's people as a whole. None of us have the complete picture. We are all just pieces in the puzzle. Only God can put them together. Jesus has placed each member in His Body; there are no separations in Him.

Why did He choose fishermen and tax collectors to change the world? The religious leaders thought they had "the truth." Only *their* traditions were right. Only *their* interpretations were inspired. *They* knew the path to God. "Who does this unordained carpenter think he is? How dare he try and teach us!"

But don't judge *them*! Most of *us* are just as bigoted, small-minded, narrow, and proud! Our endless divisions testify against us. If we didn't think that our church alone was right, why won't we work with others? Why are we so insecure if we really believe that we are part of a great and mighty army?

Our denominational pride has stifled many a move of the Spirit. What if He comes in an "unacceptable" way? (It has been said that the seven last words of the church are: "We never did it like this before!") What if *God* moves in a way that contradicts our doctrine? Will we shut *Him* out?

Listen to what Jesus said to the religious leaders of His day:

> You have a fine way of setting aside the commands of God in order to observe your own traditions. You have let go of the commands of God and are holding on to the traditions of men. (Mk. 7:9,8)

(We can't point any fingers! We have more traditions than we know.)

Jesus went out of His way to heal on the Sabbath. He broke out of the constraints of man-made rules. And when He called Himself Lord of the Sabbath, *He was proclaiming Himself Lord of every word of God made into a tradition of men.* (This is the essence of all religious traditions: "*God* said this...but *you* say that"—and we think we are helping Him out!)

Which is more sacred to us, our "order of service" or the purpose of God? Which is more important to us, keeping the people happy (especially the good tithing members!) or pleasing the Lord? If the Spirit came with tongues to "non-charismatics," would they reject their doctrine or reject the Spirit? If revival meant people "falling under the power," would people still let the power fall?

Actually, *revival always comes with religious stumbling blocks*, with divinely appointed (yet totally unasked for!) "extra's" that mean death to pride and tradition. It comes with unwelcome "bonuses" of the Spirit, something unexpected in the package.

"Lord, we're so glad for Your visitation, but who asked for all this deliverance stuff? Why are people trembling and weeping? And what's with all this speaking in tongues? Can't you send us a nice, tame, controllable outpouring that we can enjoy for a while and then leave in church?"

God does everything "decently and according to order" (1 Cor. 14:40): but according to His order, not ours! Sometimes He has to violently shake us out of *our* ways before He can get us into His way. The Bible says, "Test the spirits" (1 Jn. 4:1); it doesn't say, "Test the Spirit!" In other words, *we don't dictate to God.*

> We ought not to limit God where He has not limited Himself (Jonathan Edwards).

Our personal perferences do not matter. Our "tastes" are inconsequential. He will move how He wants to move. He refuses to be put into a religious straightjacket. *Revival belongs to God.*

It is true that revival brings division and persecution. It is true that it brings reproach and misunderstanding. And not all of this is the Spirit's doing. Sometimes people get carried away with fleshly displays; other times demonic counterfeits are passed off for the real thing. No revival is perfect. It comes through imperfect man!

But putting the flesh aside, and eliminating all Satanic manifestations, *true revival will always bring division*: it divides the hot from the cold, and the serious from the superficial. For some it is life, for others death. For some it is peace, for others a sword. Revival leaves no middle ground!

And *true revival will always bring persecution* because it will set some apart from the crowd. "How is it that the moment you are filled with the Holy Spirit persecution starts? The devil and the priests of religion will always get stirred when a man is filled with the Spirit and does things in the power of the Spirit. If you remain stationary, the devil and his agents will not disturb you much. But when you press on with God, the enemy has you as a target" (Smith Wigglesworth).

Then let's press on with God! It is far better to be a moving target that the devil is trying to shoot at than to be his stationary, captive slave! It is far better to be out of the boat, walking on the water with Jesus, than to be sitting cozy with the fear filled disciples, thinking that He is a ghost!

It's time to get out of the boat!

Chapter 11

Revival Preaching

During times of revival, everything changes. Worship becomes more real, commitment level soars, prayer abounds, soul winning increases, and true holiness becomes a way of life. The pulpit itself is transformed: both the preacher and his preaching are transfigured. A powerful new anointing flows from the Throne. God is setting things right. What are some of the marks of revival preaching?

Revival preaching is filled with divine fire. It is God shouting aloud with all His might. It is a prophetic cry to repent, revealing sin, demolishing strongholds, searching out every hiding place, and exposing man's universal guilt in the sight of a holy God. It hunts out sinners and annihilates their refuge of lies (Finney). It raises its voice like a trumpet (Is. 58:1); it is charged with the power of God (Mic. 3:8).

Revival preaching is not just skin deep! It challenges to the core and tears at the root. It reaches to the heart of hearts, leaving man no where to go but to his knees. It penetrates, provokes, and pierces; it shatters, shakes, and sears; it cuts, convicts, and confronts; it renews and it restores.

> See, I appoint you over nations and kingdoms to uproot and tear down, to destroy and overthrow, to build and to plant (Jer. 1:10).

Revival preaching produces a harvest. Its results will last a lifetime. It is so disturbing, so challenging, so searching, so probing, that it works a transformation in the very depths of a man's being. It affects a foundational change. Its "afterglow" doesn't quickly fade.

But revival preaching is not merely bringing a "hard" or "negative" message. Absolutely not! Any one can preach a negative word. Any one can minister death. *Revival preaching is life.* It flows from the heart of God. In fact, if it is true revival preaching, it must have these clear characteristics:

1) *Revival preaching must be divinely empowered.* It was said of Charles Finney that his words crashed through his listeners "like cannonballs through a basket of eggs" (Churchill). On one occasion, Finney related that:

> the word of God came through me to them in a manner that I could see was carrying all before it. It was a fire and hammer breaking the rock; and as the sword that was piercing to the dividing asunder of soul and spirit.

What was the effect on the people at such times? "If I had a sword in each hand," said Finney, "I could not have cut them off their seats as fast as they fell." It was only a matter of minutes before the whole congregation was crying out to God for mercy.

That is true revival preaching, anointed by the living Lord. It is supernatural in its working. It is clearly sent from heaven. It is unmistakably God.

2) *Revival preaching must be motivated by passion for the glory of God and compassion for a hurting world.* True revival preaching is not judgmental. It has no chip on its shoulder and no axe to grind. It carries no personal offense and holds no grudge. That is why it can be so intense: *it is caught up with the burden of God.*

In the words of Edward "Praying" Payson:

> I do not believe that my desires for revival were ever half so strong as they ought to be; nor do I see how a minister can help being in a "constant fever"...where His Master is dishonored and souls are destroyed in so many ways.

Where is the manifestation of God in this generation? Why is there no reverence for the name of the Lord? How can we allow His reputation to be dragged down? And what about the needs of the world? Who will touch the unsaved multitudes? Who will reach the hopeless and poor? Who will heal the hurting and sick? Who will set the captives free?

These are the questions on the revivalist's heart, the concerns that weigh him down. These are the burdens he carries to God, the words that combust into flame.

> Before the great revival in Gallneukirchen broke out, Martin Boos spent hours and days and often nights in lonely agonies of intercession. Afterwards, when he preached, his words were as flame and the hearts of the people as grass (D. M. McIntyre).

3) *Revival preaching must come out of a broken heart.* Before a true revivalist can preach to the crowds, he must first preach to himself. He must be stripped of all fleshly motivation to be seen or heard. He must die to all flattery and self-exalting pride. He must renounce all claims to personal fame and crucify all desires to be "somebody big." He must recognize that he is nothing and put no confidence in the flesh. Then he is ready to preach!

> The fact is when a man gets to the place where he really loves obscurity, where he does not care to preach, and where he would rather sit in the back [pew] than on the platform, then God can lift him up and use him, and not very much before (Frank Bartleman).

Do we grasp the depth of these words?

For so many today, ministry is the road to success, the way to be recognized and known by all. It means the acclaim of the crowds with the glitter and gold, the royal pastor ruling from his throne. It provides an identity in the church and in the world, as though ministry made the man.

We have gotten things totally wrong! *Ministry does not exalt the man!* Ministry means service. Ministry means being last and not first. The higher the call, the lower you must go. The grander the vision, the greater the sacrifice. And the only one to exalt is JESUS! We are to be jealous for His reputation, and His reputation alone.

> May I never boast except in the cross of our Lord Jesus Christ, through which the world has been crucified to me and I to the world (Paul, Gal. 6:14)

That is the power of a broken heart. And that is where revival preaching can begin.

4) *Revival preaching must be experiential* (in other words, you can't give what you don't have!). Look again at John the Baptist. When he preached repentance, the crowds came from everywhere and were changed (Mt. 3:1-12). He obviously "had the goods." He was preaching out of his personal experience. He was totally devoted to God. He could call on the people to do the same. He practiced what he preached. His words brought convicting fire.

Here is a crucial point: *Your public ministry can only be the natural extension of your private life.* "Ministry" is not something you do. Ministry is who you are! It is not some show you put on for the crowds or some weekly performance on Sunday. It must come from a sold-out life. It must be the articulation of everything you stand for. It must be a reflection of you.

Yet we are busy training people for "the work of the ministry" while some of their personal lives are a sham! We teach them how to produce all kinds of *outward manifestations* while many of their *inward motives* are wrong. They end up having charisma without character, power without purity, faith without fruit. How long will these "ministries" stand?

What is the solution? Is it really "either-or"? Not at all! It is "both-and": both faith and fruit; both purity and power; both character and charisma! To put it simply: *Without godly character you are disqualified from being in ministry; without God's anointing you are disqualified from doing anything once you are in ministry!* The two fit together like a hand and glove. Yet the "hand" is ours, the "glove" is God's. (In other words, you take care of your life and God will take care of the anointing.) The call flows first from the heart; the outward results will follow.

Are we separated to God and holy? Are we totally yielded to Him? Then that is a message we can preach! Are we dead to the world and its praises? Have we buried our personal pride? Then we can urge others to do the same.

But always remember: in order to freely give we first must freely receive. We can only call people into that which has truly been birthed in our lives, that which has become our constant experience, that which we will not surrender at any cost. Then we've got something to say.

And how seriously did one preacher in the 1859 Welsh revival take his responsibility?

> I would wish to preach each time as if I had to die in the pulpit when I had done preaching—as I had to go direct from the pulpit to judgment. If we are not in this frame, we shall do very little good (Humphrey Jones).

Chapter 12

The God Who Answers by Fire

If "God is one pent-up revival" (Finney), then *revival is the manifestation of God*. And if "God is a consuming fire" (Deut. 4:24), then *revival is the fire of God falling*. What happens when His flames touch the earth?

In Leviticus 9:24, when Aaron and his sons began their priestly ministry,

fire came out from the presence of the Lord and *consumed* the burnt offering and the fat portions on the altar.

In Leviticus 10:2, when Nadab and Abihu offered up unauthorized fire before the Lord,

fire came out from the presence of the Lord and *consumed* them, and they died before the Lord.

In Numbers 11:1, when the Israelites grumbled and complained,

fire from the Lord burned among them and *consumed* some of the outskirts of the camp.

And in 1 Kings 18:38, in answer to the prayer of Elijah,

> the *fire* of the Lord fell and *burned up* the sacrifice, the wood, the stones and the soil, and also licked up the water in the trench.

The fire of God always consumes something; it is always burning something up. Whether it is the sacrifice offered in righteousness or the sinner acting in presumption, the fire of God devours them both. This gives a vivid picture of the workings of the revival: the consuming, devouring fire falls in our midst! Let's see how this applies to us today.

1) Fire burns up flesh. When God comes in revival might, there is no more room for the flesh; it can't stand the presence of fire! There is no more place for "working it up," and the best plans of man go up in smoke. Proud "superstars" can not survive the withering heat, and carnal divisions drop in the ashes. For the fire of God has no favorites—if there is flesh it must be burned!

Of this you can be sure: where fleshly men predominate, revival has not yet come.

2) *A devouring fire cannot be contained.* In fact, *by its very nature*, it consumes everything that stands in its path. The more it consumes, the "hotter" it gets. Can you see the devouring Flame?

What an image of revival this is! A heaven sent, heaven empowered, heaven directed fire from God. And the Lord Himself is "fanning it into flame!"

Church program, look out! Agenda, beware! Committees, take heed! The devouring fire is near. It is burning "out of control."

3) *God's fire purifies and refines.* Malachi prophesied that the Lord would come to His people as "a refiner's fire or a launderer's soap." On that day the prophet says:

He will sit as a refiner and purifier of silver; He will purify the Levites and refine them like gold and silver" (Mal. 3:2-3).

He will pass His priestly servants through the flames, melting all impurities out with His heat. Ouch!

Have you ever been refined in God's furnace? Have you experienced the heat of His flames? Has your dross risen up to the surface—filthy, ugly, and proud—so that God could skim it off? Have you been shocked to see how much flesh was still there—impurities and imperfections of every kind— before the intense fire of God's visitation melted it away?

No one likes to talk about sin. No one wants to be "negative." But God has a higher purpose. He doesn't want to concentrate on the negative. He wants to remove it! He wants us to add to our "righteousness consciousness" a depth of "righteousness conduct." He wants to conform us to the image of Messiah, in thought, in word, and in deed. *He wants to make us pure.*

Listen to the words of the great apostle of faith, Smith Wigglesworth:

If you are to be really reconstructed, it will be a hard time...not in a singing meeting, but when you think there is no hope for you...tried by fire...God purges, takes the dross away, and brings forth pure gold. Only melted gold is minted.

What was Wigglesworth's own experience? How did he walk in such a degree of the love and power of God? This was his personal testimony:

> Before God could bring me to this place He broke me a thousand times. I have wept, I have groaned, I have travailed many a night until God broke me. It seems to me that until God has mowed you down you never can have this longsuffering for others.

> There have been times when I have been pressed through circumstances and it seemed as if a dozen railroad engines were going over me, but I have found that the hardest things are just lifting places into the grace of God.

If you've never been "burned," get ready, because this is what revival is about. *It is only the scorched ones He can use.*

4) *When the fire falls, it is totally consuming.* 1 Kings 18:38 is especially clear: God's fire consumed the sacrifice, the wood, the *stone* altar and the *water*. Nothing was left. God took it all. The flames licked it up—every drop!

And this is the experience of revival: your life is devoured by God. You cease to be your own. You experience divine constraint. The passions of God consume you, and zeal for His house eats you up. Your every thought is "the Lord" and you are possessed by the fire of God. You are dominated by the Spirit, and carried along by His wind. The demands of heaven are upon you.

Revival is intense! If you are determined to follow Him at a distance, then revival is not for you.

5) *Fire begets fire.* Not only does fire consume. Fire spreads. In fact, fire reproduces itself, since *everything it touches turns to flame.*

Ezekiel describes a fiery angelic figure sent forth from the throne of God:

From what appeared to be his waist down he was like fire, and from there up his appearance was as bright as glowing metal (Ezek. 8:2).

Why was the angel "like fire"? Because He came forth from the presence of the One who is wholly Fire! God makes "his servants flames of fire" (Heb. 1:7). The fire falls to make us like Him.

How can you avoid becoming cold and lukewarm? How can you stay on fire? Walk with the Lord. Stay close by His side. He *is* the Fire.

6) *Where there is no fire, there is no glory.* When the glory of God is present, people know it. There is no more need to announce the presence of God's glory than there is need to announce the presence of fire. *God's glory is something tangible.* Everyone feels it; everyone sees it; everyone experiences it. In fact, *the glory of God is the visible manifestation of God*, either by a distinct outward form (like the pillar of cloud), or by a supernatural outward demonstration (like the raising of Lazarus from the dead, or a totally miraculous healing). What has become of the glory?

Because our generation has experienced no sweeping revival, we have "exchanged the glory of the immortal God for images made to look like mortal men" (Rom. 1:23). We have cheapened it, trivialized it, and made it something light (the Hebrew for glory means "heavy"!). We have had plenty of smoke (we can really talk it up!) but very little fire.

How will we know when the glory appears? How can we see the glory of God?

> While Aaron was speaking to the whole Israelite community, they *looked* toward the desert, and there was the glory *appearing* in the cloud (Ex. 16:10).
>
> *To the Israelites the glory of the Lord looked like a consuming fire on top of the mountain* (Ex. 24:16).
>
> Didn't I say to you that if you would believe you would see the glory of God? (These are the words of Jesus!—Jn. 11:40)

Believe His Word. Then you will *see*. Show us your glory oh God! (Ex. 33:18)

7) *The baptism in the Holy Spirit is a baptism in fire.* You can not choose between the Spirit and the fire. They are inseparable, one and the same. There are not *two* baptisms, one "in the spirit" and the other "in fire." There is one baptism only *in the Spirit and fire* (Mt. 3:11).

When the Holy Spirit came on the Day of Pentecost, He arrived with tongues of fire. One hundred and twenty men and women were divinely empowered and supernaturally endued. Heaven's power invaded the earth. And those 120 then shook their whole world.

What have we received today? We've got plenty of tongues, but almost no fire; plenty of formulas, but almost no flames. We are high on utterance, but low on unction. Where is the holy heat of His presence?

Sure, we've moved beyond the days of hopeless "tarrying" meetings; we've discarded the abominable practice of:

"Repeat after me." We are much more sophisticated now. We've reduced God to a guaranteed method! "Just follow my instructions and you'll get the Spirit! It's so easy to receive today!"

Contrast all this with the experience of John Lake at the turn of this century. See what happened after God said to him: "You are now baptized in the Holy Spirit."

> Currents of power began to rush through my being from the crown of my head to the soles of my feet. The shocks of power increased in rapidity and voltage. As these currents of power would pass through me, they seemed to come upon my head, rush through my body and through my feet into the floor. The power was so great that my body began to vibrate intensely so that I believe if I had not been sitting in such a deep low chair I might have fallen to the floor.

And how did a fellow minister with whom Lake was praying discover that Lake had been immersed in the Spirit? They were about to pray for a sick woman. Lake touched the tips of his fingers on the top of her head. The other minister took her by the hand. Lake describes it from there:

> At the instant their hands touched, a flash of dynamic power went through the sick woman, and as my friend held her hand the shock of power went through her hand into him. The rush of power into his person was so great that it caused him to fall on the floor. He looked up at me with joy and surprise, and springing to his feet said, "Praise the Lord, John, Jesus has baptized you with the Holy Ghost!"

That is the Spirit of God! Yet today we have to tell the people themselves that they have received the Spirit! If we don't tell them they don't even know it!

Let me be painfully honest. *If there is any area where we have insulted and belittled the power of God it is in the area of the baptism in the Holy Spirit.* What has happened to the "mighty baptism from on high"? How many have been *immersed*—soaked, saturated, dunked, and virtually drowned—in His enabling power and might? Where is the overwhelming flood tide of His waves in America today?

Yes—thank God for tongues! Pray in tongues, sing in tongues, speak in tongues every hour of the night and day. *But don't stop there.* Ask God for the fire of the Spirit; believe Him for the Spirit on fire.

Before God's throne there are seven lamps blazing. "These are the seven spirits of God" (Rev. 4:5). The Spirit continues to burn.

8) *There is an eternal, unquenchable fire.* Nothing unholy can survive God's judgment flames. Nothing wicked can endure. The Lord of the harvest will burn up "the chaff with unquenchable fire" (Mt. 3:12); "the weeds" will be "pulled up and burned" (Mt. 13:40). On that day, Jesus will be revealed from heaven "in blazing fire," punishing with everlasting destruction those who do not know God and do not obey the gospel (2 Thess. 1:7-9). *Only the righteous will stand.*

> The sinners in Zion are terrified; trembling grips the godless: "Who of us can dwell with the *consuming fire*? Who of us can dwell with *everlasting burning*?" He who walks righteously and speaks what is right, who rejects gain from extortion and keeps his hand from accepting bribes, who stops his ears against plots of murder and shuts his eyes

against contemplating evil—this is the man who will dwell on the heights (Is. 33:14-16).

He has been refined in the crucible; he is now impervious to the flame; *he can live in the presence of God.*

Are you ready for the fire? Then you're ready for revival. But what will be devoured when it comes?

> "As I looked, thrones were set in place,
> and the Ancient of Days took His seat.
> His clothing was as white as snow;
> the hair of His head was white like wool.
>
> His throne was flaming with fire
> and its wheels all ablaze.
> A river of fire was flowing,
> coming out before Him.
>
> Thousands upon thousands attended Him;
> Ten thousand times ten thousand
> stood before Him.
>
> THE COURT WAS SEATED, AND THE
> BOOKS WERE OPENED" (Daniel 7:9-10).

And then...?

Chapter 13

The End of the American Gospel Enterprise

What began as a movement in Jerusalem became a philosophy in Greece, an institution in Rome, a culture in Europe, and an enterprise in America (Anonymous).

Do you sense the Spirit's pain?

Consider the sins of our great American gospel machine.

We have sold the Son of God for profit and marketed the Holy Spirit for gain. We have merchandized the Word for money and turned the anointing into a commodity. Preaching the gospel is now big business—our spiritual executives grow fat while the hungry sheep go unfed.

What will our holy God do?

We have made the ministry into an industry and the church into a corporate name. Instead of revival we have revenue. Big profits are up; true prophets are down.

Come and see what we have done.

Consider today's Christian music scene. How much personal wealth has been amassed? Attend some big concerts and look all around. The superstars sing while the crowds scream their names. Can God be pleased with all this? Are there "idols unaware" in our midst?

"Your attitude should be the same as that of Messiah Jesus...who did not come to be served, but to serve" (Phil. 2:5; Mt. 20:28). Is that where we are today? There is so much stardom and so little sacrifice, so many entertainers and so few examples, so much of Hollywood and so little of heaven. Performance is high, purity is low. But the story gets worse from here.

Our obsession with media has produced a monstrosity. We have birthed a new breed of top heavy ministries, and many preachers have lost sight of their calls. The weekly bills have mounted, and financial demands become great. So instead of feeding there is pleading: "Help keep our gospel ship afloat!" But as dollars increase, so do those who spend them (see Eccles. 5:11), and there is never an end to the need.

Have you ever wondered how much spiritual return you are getting on your money? For every dollar given to some major media ministries, how many lives are really transformed? With millions spent daily, where is the harvest? With marketing galore, where is the fruit? Have we forgotten that it is only the blessing of God that produces a crop, and He can work with many or few? *Greater media exposure does not guarantee greater results.*

Look outside of the United States. Why do some home churches in Communist China accomplish more in a month without media or money than many of our mega-congregations accomplish in a year? Because they are sold out to Jesus and dead to the world, and they live for souls and the Lord. And that is truly the Gospel. That is God's way to succeed. But the more we depend on our earthly endeavors, the less of God's help we will see.

We have laid the trap for ourselves! Consider how we have been snared. We make our "ministers" famous and exalt them to celebrity status. Now they need to go on the air! But they are too simple, unpolished, so they must learn the new rules of this game. They must become suave and professional; their message must bring in the crowds. Success is now measured by the ratings; daily prayers are lifted up for the funds. The best marketing agents are hired, and production crews grow and abound. But little by little the anointing has left; the Spirit didn't fit in the show!

Do we see how our hyper-professionalism reeks of the arm of flesh? Do we recognize how far we have fallen from the "simplicity of the Messiah"? We have exchanged soul-winning for showmanship and passed up travail for talent. Once we had powerful ministries, challenging us with the Word. Now we have multi-media extravaganzas, and even sinners find them fun. Salesmanship is at an all time high, salvation at a relative low.

Look at how much things have changed. Consider the example of Paul. He did not peddle the Word for profit; he did not market shoddy goods for gain (2 Cor. 2:17). But today we are filled with new gimmicks: "Will it sell?" is the name of the game.

Paul told the Corinthians that he was "poor, yet making many rich; having nothing, yet possessing everything" (2 Cor. 6:10). Some of our leaders have gotten it backwards! *They* are rich—and making many poor (the contributions of the needy have financed their affluent life-styles); *they* have everything—yet possess nothing (they live in material plenty while their lives are spiritually poor). How gross in God's eyes this must seem!

We have milked the Body for money and used His Word to stake our claims. We have mastered the "free-will" offering with "deals" no one could refuse. And we have appealed to man's greediest motives, promising instant "hundred-fold returns." Paul spoke of men with corrupt minds who "think that godliness is a means to financial gain" (1 Tim. 6:5). How much longer can this go on?

God is saddened by our enterprising mentality, our get rich on the gospel approach. Do you hear Him quietly weeping? He is heartsick and filled with grief. Is there nothing sacred any more?

We have given, we have prayed, we have waited and believed for so long. But we have done it all for ourselves! We have learned to live like king's kids—unmoved by the cries of the poor! We have learned to succeed and prosper—oblivious to the suffering of the world! We sit insulated and hardened to missions, yet entranced by the TV's warm glow. Our senses are dull. Our hearts are cold. *We live too far from the cross.*

Our funds have been spent on our own edification and our energies devoted to build up our lives. We are stuffed with new revelation and gorged with the hottest new truth. Yet instead of getting healthy, we're fat; instead of getting stronger, we're stale!

We are specialists in praise and worship, and experts on interpretive dance. Apostles and prophets are again in our midst, and Word-teachers fill our whole land. But the "old-time power" is missing and divine visitation is rare. The blessing of God is departing and we are left with a great big game.

Our ship has set sail, its decks are all full, but the wind of the Spirit has waned.

Listen to the Word of the Lord:

Give careful thought to your ways. You have planted much, but have harvested little. You eat, but never have enough. You drink, but never have your fill. You put on clothes, but are not warm. You earn wages, only to put them in a purse with holes in it. You expected much, but see, it turned out to be little. What you brought home, I blew it away (Hag. 1:5-9).

What a picture of the American Church!

The gospel show is now over
and its businesses beginning to close.

The gospel firm is folding
and its industries shutting their doors.

The gospel ship is sinking.

We've come to the end of the dream.

Chapter 14

Is It Too Late for America?

Is God through with America? Is He ready to spew us out of His mouth? Is it too late for revival? Is our country destined to die?

Maybe not! We have definite proof that He is beginning to move. *He is judging the house of God.* He is bringing us down before He lifts us up and smiting before He heals. *Revival could be at the door.*

Sometimes great revival precedes great judgment, and other times great judgment precedes great revival. *Revival and judgment go hand in hand.* We stand somewhere in that cycle today.

Twenty-five hundred years ago, the young king Josiah turned to God with all his heart. He led the nation of Judah in genuine repentance. Mercy was poured out. And then, after Josiah's death in battle, judgment began to fall (2 Kings 22-25). Why did revival come before judgment?

In revival, God is extending His goodness in a totally supernatural fashion. He is going completely "out of His way" to bless and change lives. He is giving people unusual opportunities to receive His love. He is giving them one great last chance. *Revival means super-abounding grace.*

But revival means "higher stakes"—"from everyone who has been given much, much will be demanded" (Lk. 12:48). When people refuse to accept God's gracious offer, they are judged more strictly. That's why Jesus said that it would be worse for Korazin, Bethsaida and Capernaum than for Tyre, Sidon and Sodom—because those cities had seen the Lord and His miracles, yet still they refused to repent (Mt. 11:20-24).

Revival is God's hand of love extended. Judgment is His offer refused.

But what about when the opposite occurs? Why does judgment often precede revival?

An un-revived church is a church in sin. It is carnal and cold, proud and deficient. And if this is the condition of the saved, what must the state of the unsaved be like? A visitation is clearly needed, so believers begin to seek the Lord. But what will He do when He comes? He will come to clean us up!

> See, I will send My messenger, who will prepare the way before Me. Then suddenly the Lord you are seeking will come to His temple…But who can endure the day of His coming? Who can stand when He appears? For He will be like a refiner's fire or a launderer's soap (Mal. 3:1-3).

God Himself comes in answer to our prayers!

Many times, when judgment comes, people begin to repent. When things get bad people turn to God. They can no longer trust in earthly treasures, they can no longer depend on the arm of flesh. They recognize the fleeting and unstable nature of this world—they have nowhere to look but up. So the first step to revival is often the purging, humbling, judgment of God—and the purging starts with us!

"For it is time for judgment to begin with the family of God"; then He will judge the world (1 Pet. 4:17-18). He wants to make us acceptable in His sight.

> *Then* the Lord will have men who will bring offerings in righteousness (Mal. 3:3).

But where do we fit in this scheme today?

Clearly, *America is being judged.* Corruption is being exposed in the church and in the world. (This is only the tip of the iceberg. There is much, much more to come!) Our economy is reeling and tottering, and we are dependent on foreign banks. We are held hostage by the nations, and we have decreasing international clout. Even America's natural beauty is being marred—from the vast forest fires at Yellowstone, our most famous national park, to the massive oil spill in Cape Valdez, spoiling our last wilderness frontier. The shaking of God is here.

But in spite of the hardships, this is good news! *Revival is on the way.* Stop and consider the facts.

We are not experiencing the judgment that *follows* revival—revival has not yet come. No! This is the judgment that *precedes* revival—the fire before the flood. This is the necessary pain before the power, the required shaking before the shower. God is on the move!

In answer to the prayers of thousands of His children, in response to the fasting and brokenness of so many saints, the Lord has finally begun to act. He is intervening in our affairs. He has said, "Enough is enough."

Don't you see how exciting this is? God is revealing sin in the camp; He wants to move us on.

Consecrate yourselves, for tomorrow the Lord will do amazing things among you (Josh. 3:5).

Go to the people and consecrate them today and tomorrow. Have them wash their clothes and be ready by the third day, because on that day the Lord will come down on Mount Sinai in the sight of all the people (Ex. 19:10-11).

Even the priests, who approach the Lord [that's us!], must consecrate themselves or the Lord will break out against them (Ex. 19:22).

God is preparing us for His coming—His coming right into our midst. This is something to shout about! But will we be ready when He comes?

Look at Paul's words in Acts 17:30. Speaking of God's dealings with the idol-worshiping Gentiles, he says:

In the past God overlooked such ignorance, but now He commands all people everywhere to repent.

This can be applied to the American church of the last two decades. Much of today's sin has been here for years. We were guilty then, and we are guilty now. But what God seemed to "overlook" then, He is not overlooking now. He is calling us to repent.

He is bringing to light the things that were hidden. He is confronting us with our wrongs. He is revealing our spiritual poverty. He is counseling us to "deal" with Him (Rev. 3:18).

> I counsel you to buy from Me gold refined in the fire, so you can become rich [this stands for true spirituality and godliness, instead of instant formulas and methods]; and white clothes to wear, so you can cover your shameful nakedness [i.e., deep purity of heart and holiness of life in place of worldliness and carnality]; and salve to put on your eyes, so you can see [a spirit of revelation to show us just who and where we really are today]. Those whom I love I rebuke and discipline. So be earnest and repent. Here I am! I stand at the door and knock. If anyone hears My voice and opens the door, I will come in and eat with him, and he with Me (Rev. 3:18-20).

This is the grace of God. The church most soundly reproved in the book of Revelation is given the most special promise. Restored fellowship is being offered. *Jesus stands at the door.*

The final chapter has not yet been written. The verdict is not yet in. America stands in the balance. The judgments have already begun. Will we live or will we die?

Hear the Word of the Lord:

> "Even now," declares the Lord, "return to Me with all your heart, with fasting and weeping and mourning." Rend your heart and not your garments. Return to the Lord your God, for He is gracious and compassionate, slow to anger and

abounding in love, and He relents from sending calamity. *Who knows?* He may turn and have pity and leave behind a blessing—grain offerings and drink offerings for the Lord your God (Joel 2:12-14).

Who knows? The best could be yet to come.

Chapter 15

Fall on Your Face and Pray!

How can we turn things around? How can we get out of the deep rut? What is the answer for those who have not grown spiritually for many months and years? What must we do to change?

We must desire God more than anything else. We must seek Him, and cry out to Him, and long for Him. We must make an absolute determination that nothing will separate us from Him. We must be utterly ruthless with ourselves and cut away everything that offends. *It is time to put away our idols!*

When God told Jacob to return to Bethel and build Him an altar there, Jacob said to his household:

Get rid of the foreign gods you have with you, and purify yourselves and change your clothes (Gen. 35:2).

But why were foreign gods there at all?

Jacob had met with God once at Bethel and entered into a covenant with Him there (Gen. 28). But that was a long time ago! The Lord had kept up His part of the agreement; Jacob had let things slip. For years, He had let his family and servants worship foreign gods. He had allowed them to have divided hearts. Now God was ready to visit him again. The idols had to go!

Isn't that just like us? We have our "Bethel" experiences and powerfully meet with God (like Jacob in Gen. 28). We make a covenant to live for Him and Him alone. And then life goes on. The old habits begin to come back. The flesh starts to rule again. We witness less, pray less, and fast less. (We are supposed to be growing!) Our hearts no longer break for the sick and destitute. And then God says, "Go back to Bethel and worship Me there!"

All of a sudden we wake up. We take inventory of our lives and are shocked. We have been living according to the desires of the flesh. We have hardly denied ourselves at all. *Jesus is our limited Lord.* Sometimes we're even ashamed of Him.

We look at ourselves and grow sad. We remember how real God was to us. But now our eyes are on others. We work for the praise of man and are paralyzed by the fear of man. We seek to please people more than we seek to please God. Human words influence us more than divine words, and we are satisfied in this world. *Our lives have been filled with idols.* And God is saying, "It's time to go back to Bethel. I'm ready to meet with you there."

How should we respond?

We must fall on our faces and pray. We must make a radical change in our schedules. Shut off the TV and the VCR. (Television is the number one polluting force among American believers today.) Put down the newspaper and the magazines. Cut out the endless hours of phone call chatter. Seek the face of God.

Nothing is more important. Nothing will do you more good. Desire God in prayer. Tell Him your frustration. Confess to Him your sin. Turn to God with your heart. He *will* turn to you.

The devil says, "It's too late. Just quit. God will never hear. Maybe He will bless the others, but it's way too late for you."

Don't listen to the devil's lies! He knows you're on the right track. He's making the last ditch attempt to stop you. Spend *more time* with God! The devil is a thief.

The world has not yet seen what God can do through a person completely dedicated to Him (D. L. Moody).

There are no secret methods or magical tricks. *Fervent prayer is the key.* It opens us up to God. It invites Him to work in our lives. It exposes us to His presence. Something has to give.

Draw near to God and He will draw near to you (Jas. 4:8). That is a promise of the Word. Wherever you are, whatever your condition, prayer can carry you back. Just move in God's direction. Every day, take a step. Skip some meals and devour the Word. Fast and shut yourself in with Jesus. Call out to Him every hour—morning, noon and

night. Pour out your soul to God! Before you know it, he
will change your heart. *It is absolutely sure.*

> Let us acknowledge the Lord; let us press on to acknowledge
> Him. As surely as the sun rises He will appear; He will come
> to us like the winter rains, like the spring rains that water
> the earth (Hos. 6:3)

The Spirit is on your side. Jesus intercedes on your be-
half. The Father longs to bless you. What can hold you
back? Cast discouragement aside; put hopelessness under
your feet. Make a determination. Seek the Lord with all of
your strength. He will not let you down.

> No matter what your soul may be coveting, if it becomes the
> supreme cry of your life, not the secondary matter, or the
> third or fourth, the fifth, or tenth, but the supreme desire of
> your soul, the paramount issue—all the powers and energies
> of your spirit, soul and body are reaching out and crying to
> God for the answer—it is going to come! (John Lake)

Mothers at home with young children—you can meet
with Him there! Keep the Word open all day. Look at it
when you pass by. Let your heart cry go up to the throne.
He will take notice and hear.

God's presence is not limited to church buildings! You
can experience Him right on your job. He is looking at the
longings of your soul. Spiritual hunger is a state of the
heart. *Let your thoughts be consumed with the Lord.*

No one is too busy to seek His face! We have time to
worry. We have time to relax. We have time for friends. *We
have time for God.* None of us are too busy to eat and drink

and sleep. *None of us are too busy to pray.* And God is not too busy to answer!

> If from there you seek the Lord your God, you will find Him if you look for Him with all your heart and with all your soul (Deut. 4:29).

He has bound Himself by His Word.

Do God's will today. Tomorrow never comes. Follow His leading this hour. Forget about falling short. He will guide you one step at a time.

Humble yourself in the sight of the Lord and He will lift you up (Jas. 4:10). Depend upon the grace of God. He will deliver, and He will keep. If you seek Him with all your heart, you will never have a regret.

And what happens when you get so hungry that you are determined to see revival come, whatever it takes, whatever the cost, whatever the consequences may be?

Ninety years ago "Daddy" Seymour became desperate for more of God. He had heard from Charles Parham about the baptism in the Spirit, and he was bent on receiving from heaven. He was working as a waiter and pastoring a church. Yet for two and a half years he prayed five hours a day. Seymour relates:

> I got to Los Angeles, and there the hunger was not less but more. I prayed, "God, what can I do?" The Spirit said, "Pray more. There are better things to be had in spiritual life, but they must be sought out with faith and prayer." "But Lord, I am praying five hours a day now." I increased my hours of prayer to seven, and prayed on for a year and a half more. I prayed to God to give me what Parham preached, the real

Holy Ghost and fire and tongues and love and power of God like the apostles had.

John Lake tells us the end of the story:

God had put such a hunger into that man's heart that when the fire of God came it glorified him. I do not believe any other man in modern times had a more wonderful deluge of God in his life than God gave that dear fellow, and the glory and power of a real Pentecost swept the world.

It was the Azusa Street outpouring!

Seymour preached to Lake's congregation of ten thousand people,

when the glory and power of God was upon his spirit, and men shook and trembled and cried to God.

That is what God did through a sold-out vessel. Will you sell out for Him today?

Chapter 16

The Revival to End All Revivals

God is going to move across this planet one last time. There will a final outpouring of the Spirit that will supersede all previous outpourings. The last great revival will come and the whole earth will be affected. Only God's Kingdom will remain.

The Lord will shake the heavens and the earth (Heb. 12:25-29). Everything man-made will fall; human empires will totter and crumble. God's people will stand back in awe. He will visit this earth again.

All the revivals combined will not equal this great and mighty move. This final revival will impact the world. It will be the visible display of the glory of the Lord. It will touch every part of the globe.

The gospel will be preached to all peoples (Mt. 24:14), and the nations will be harvested in mass (Rev. 7:9-14). Multitudes of Jews will be swept into the Kingdom (Zech. 12:10-13:1;

Dan. 12:1), and Israel itself will be saved (Rom. 11:26; Is. 60:21). God's splendor will be seen worldwide (Is. 40:5).

The end of this age will be a time of parallel extremes (Rev. 22:11). The wheat and the tares will be fully grown (Mt. 13:36-43). Righteousness will flourish and wickedness will abound (Dan. 12:10; Mt. 24:12). The people of God will rise higher into glory while the world sinks deeper into sin (Is. 60:1-2). Many will fall away, yet many others will be saved. The blood of the martyrs will run deep because the people of God will be alive!

A universal revival will come! The early and the late rains will both fall in the first month of the season (Joel 2:23, NKJV). Overnight a harvest will be planted and reaped. What used to take a year will take only days. God will accelerate the pace (Is. 60:22)! *And after that,* He will pour out His Spirit on all flesh (Joel 2:28). Can you imagine the tidal wave of God?

There will be a demonstration of God's power in the heavens and on the earth. Every foundation will be shaken. A time of testing will come to all men (Rev. 3:10), but the righteous will not be moved (Ps. 15).

This skeptical age will end under a flood of God's miracle power. Satan's counterfeits will be exposed and his people be cast down. God's holy arm will be revealed and His children will gather around. Then Jesus will appear for every eye to see. What a fitting climax to the final revival! It will be a visitation for real.

The destruction of the wicked will be so thorough (Mt. 13:41-42; 2 Thess. 1:7-9) and the outpouring of the Spirit so widespread that "the earth will be filled with the knowledge of the glory of the Lord as the waters cover the sea" (Hab. 2:14).

> Many peoples will go and say, 'Come, let us go up to the Mount of the Lord, to the House of the God of Jacob; that He may instruct us in His ways, and that we may walk in His paths.' For instruction shall come forth from Zion, the Word of the Lord from Jerusalem. Thus He will judge among the nations and arbitrate for the many peoples. And they shall beat their swords into plowshares and their spears into pruning hooks: Nation shall not take up sword against nation; they shall never again know war (Is. 2:3-4, New Jewish Version).

On earth God's heavenly will shall be done! Glory and praise to His name!

We could live to see it all. Suffering could end before our eyes; sickness and grief could cease. Starvation and pain could disappear and the presence of God fill the earth.

> *This could be the final hour.*
> The Lord's coming is so very near!

***

We stand today at the beginning of the end. We approach the first month of the last harvest season. It is the beginning of the final reaping. The day of reckoning has come.

> Now is the time to live for God,
> to yield your all to Him.

Now is the time to completely sell out,
to make your life count for Him.

This is the time and this is the hour.

What you sow this day will last forever.

"TODAY IF YOU HEAR HIS VOICE,
DO NOT HARDEN YOUR HEART."

References

Pages 1-2—Sources for the statistics referred to include: Federal Bureau of Investigation Uniform Crime Reports for 1988; U.S. Department of Health and Human Services, 1988 National Household Survey on Drug Abuse; U.S. Senate Report on Child Pornography and Pedophilia (1980); The National Coalition Against Pornography.

Pages 3-4—For the description of Sardis, see Robert H. Mounce, *The Book of Revelation* (Eerdmans, 1977), pp. 109-110.

Page 7—Charles G. Finney, *Lectures on Revivals of Religion* (Revell, N.D.), pp. 1-2.

Page 11—The New York Mills factory revival account is cited by Basil Miller, *Charles Finney* (Bethany, N.D.), p. 54.

Page 23—The Scripture quotations are taken from: Mark 1:15; Luke 13:3, 24:47; Acts 2:38, 17:30.

Pages 29—Joseph Parker, quoted by Leonard Ravenhill, *Why Revival Tarries* (Bethany, 1962), p. 98.

Page 29—Frank Bartleman, *Another Wave of Revival* (Whittaker, 1982), p. 10.

Page 33—For the account of Evan Roberts, see Elfion Evans, *The Welsh Revival of 1904* (Evangelical Press of Wales, 1969), pp. 68-71.

Page 36—William T. Stead, quoted by Winkie Pratney, *Revival* (Whittaker, 1983), p. 194 (his emphasis).

Pages 38-39—For the account from the Welsh revival of 1859, see Thomas Phillips, *The Welsh Revival* (Banner of Truth, 1989), p. 12.

Pages 39-40—Arthur Wallis, *Revival, The Rain from Heaven* (Revell, 1979), pp. 50-51.

Page 40—Benjamin Franklin quoted by John Pollock, *George Whitefield and the Great Awakening* (Lion Publishing, 1972), p. 121.

Page 43—For the accounts of the Cane Ridge Revival, see Mary Stuart Relfe, *The Cure of All Ills* (League of Prayer, 1988), pp. 33-34.

Page 44—Mary Stuart Relfe, *The Cure of All Ills*, p. 49.

Page 47—D. Martyn Lloyd-Jones, *Revival* (Crossway, 1987), p. 47.

Page 47—Jonathan Edwards, quoted by Pratney, *Revival* p. 114.

Page 50—Marietta Davis, *Scenes Beyond the Grave*, ed. Gordon Lindsay (Christ for the Nations, 1980), p. 27.

Page 50—Elfion Evans,*The Welsh Revival of 1904*, pp. 77-78.

Page 54—Frank Bartleman, *Another Wave of Revival*, p. 41.

Page 57—Jonathan Edwards, *Jonathan Edwards on Revival* (Banner of Truth, 1987), p. 89.

Page 57—Smith Wigglesworth, *Ever Increasing Faith* (rev. ed., Gospel Publishing House, 1971), pp. 105-106.

Page 60—Churchill, quoted by Lewis A. Drummond, *The Life and Ministry of Charles Finney* (Bethany, 1983), p. 62 (see also pp. 71-72 and p. 76).

Page 61—Edward Payson, quoted by Henry C. Fish, *Handbook of Revivals* (Gano Books, 1988), p. vi.

Pages 61-62—D. M. McIntyre, quoted by Ravenhill, *Why Revival Tarries*, p. 16.

Page 62—Frank Bartleman, *Another Wave of Revival* p. 129.

Page 64—Humphrey Jones, quoted by Phillips, *The Welsh Revival*, p. 10.

Pages 67-68—Smith Wigglesworth, quoted by Jack Hywel-Davies, *The Life of Smith Wigglesworth* (Vine Books, 1988), pp. 149-150; and Smith Wigglesworth, *Ever Increasing Faith*, pp. 151 and 21.

Pages 71-72—For the account of John Lake's baptism in the Spirit, see *The John G. Lake Sermons on Dominion over Demons, Disease and Death*, ed. Gordon Lindsay (Christ for the Nations, 1982), pp. 6-7.

Pages 90-92—John G. Lake, *Spiritual Hunger and other Sermons*, ed. Gordon Lindsay (Christ for the Nations, 1987), pp. 7,13-14.

MESSIAH BIBLICAL INSTITUTE
&
GRADUATE SCHOOL OF THEOLOGY
ALIVE WITH THE FIRE OF GOD!

* Do you need further training for the work of the ministry?

* Are you looking for a school with a burden for revival and a passion for world missions?

* Would you like to study in a personalized environment that emphasizes integrity in leadership and the importance of the local church?

* Do you want to learn from a highly qualified faculty grounded in serious study of the Word?

* Are you looking for a training center that is sensitive to the Jewish roots of the faith and God's eternal covenant with Israel?

* Do you desire an atmosphere of prayer and freedom in the Spirit?

* Would you like to work toward a college or graduate degree without compromising your faith?

Then contact MESSIAH BIBLICAL INSTITUTE today and ask about our intensive ministry training and degree programs. Call 301-330-6006, or write to: Registrar, Messiah Biblical Institute, P.O. Box 7163, Gaithersburg, MD 20898.

* * * *

If you can't join us in person, then inquire about our specialized CORRESPONDENCE SCHOOL. You can earn a certificate or work toward a degree in the privacy of your own home! Classes include:

Answering Jewish objections to Jesus/ How to Study God's Word/ I Am the Lord Your Healer/ The Messiah in Jewish Tradition/ Israel, the Church and the Last Days/ Apologetics/ The Sermon on the Mount

Write or call today for further information.